#DEARFUTUREWIFE

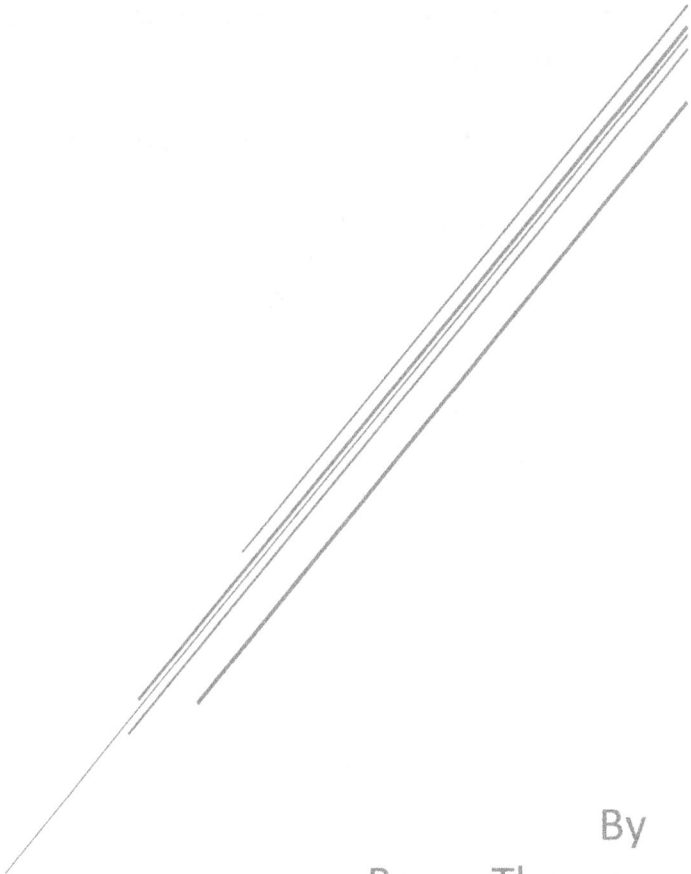

By
Bryan Thomas

Printed in the United States of America

First Printing, 2015

ISBN 13:978-0-9882987-8-1

Alegna Media Publishing,LLC

Acknowledgements

I would first like to thank the Lord Jesus Christ for the completion of this amazing journey and the strength to write even when I felt like giving up.

To my parents, Benjamin Thomas and Erma Thomas, my two sisters Robyn Thomas, Jillian Thomas and the Rivers Family as a whole for the support you have rendered to my in all my endeavors.

To my best friend, Tiffany Michelle Thompson, thank you for your love, your support and your prayers. You have no idea how much this moment means to me, I can't wait to see you and my Zoe very soon. I love you so much.

To the Mays family, thank you for your unwavering support over the last 4 years.

To my extend family of brothers, William May, Henry Young, Dominick White, Brian Carson, James Bryant, Andre Carroll, Georedt Huggins, Courtney Ford, William Harrell, Deangelo Snow, Joshua Johnson, Jason Johnson and Alex Ware.

To my extended family of sisters, Trina Washington, Malika Sanders, Belinda Oliver, Angel Chisolm, Dr Candis Hill, Dakita Gaspaire, Kesha Mcgee, Ori Williams, Britney Thorne, Myeshia Daniels, Danielle Agge-Burnette, Kristy

Waldburg,Bonita Jackson, Amber Reese, Christina Chianumba and Jennifer Dumas.

 To every reader, supporter and follower of this vision, thank you so much I am humbled even now, as I watch the dream that seemed so far away now completed.

 Special Thanks to Marquis Hall for the amazing illustration on the cover of this book.

A very big thank you to the great visionary Angela Stevenson of AES Productions and Alegna Media Publishing, for helping bring this vision to pass.

This is just the beginning!

 Bryan Thomas

TABLE OF CONTENTS

CHAPTER
1

THE FOUNDATION   2

CHAPTER
2

THE RESPONSIBILITY   19

CHAPTER 3-

THE COMMITMENT   29

CHAPTER
4

THE CONNECTION   39

CHAPTER
5

THE STORIES   48

CHAPTER
6

THE MEMORIES   58

CHAPTER
7

THE PROMISE   67

CHAPTER
8

THE PRAYERS   75

CHAPTER
9

TRUE LOVE FOREVER   83

Preface

First and foremost I want to thank God for every woman who will read this book. This has truly been a 4-year journey, many days I wanted to give up but here I am. To every woman that will read this book, I pray that you are inspired, enlightened and even begin to release anything that will hold you back from being the amazing woman you truly are.

My hope is that this book will lead you to truly reveal the beautiful future wife that you will become one day soon.

As you prepare to turn the pages, remember that God created you to be loved by the right man. Whether you're single and healing or completely broken for your past relationships, know that you are worth so much.

You deserve to be loved by the man who God created just for you, may your heart be filled with the expectation and the anticipation of the joy that you will receive as you embrace the title of #FutureWife.

You are not only a beautiful woman but you are so valuable to the world. You will be found by not just a good man, but the right man and he will show you the love that you were intended to truly have in your life. This book is not just for the women who desire to be a Future Wife, but this is also for the future mothers and even the current mothers who are waiting to be found by the man who has the right combination to unlock your heart's desire to be loved and cherished.

Let this letter be the beginning of you becoming the amazing woman that you already are. Now before you even begin reading recite these words. My name is *(Your name)* and I am an amazing future wife in the making, am not a product of my past or my mistakes but I am being the journey of becoming the best future wife to my future husband. I am beautiful, I am dynamic, I am a great wife and my future marriage to my husband will help launch me into my purpose. Once again thank you for reading, #YoursTruly

*Happy is the man who finds a true friend,
and far happier is he who finds that true
friend in his wife.*

Franz Schubert

1

<u>Chapter 1- The Foundation</u>

#DearFutureWife

With this ring, I vow to cherish every memory, moment and value the precious time that I will spend next to you. This is the beginning of something so beautiful and looking into your eyes for a lifetime is an adventure I can't wait to experience. I won't promise you every day will be perfect, but I do promise that I am committed to what the future holds between you and I. I will leave you with no doubt that my heart is only committed to you

I love you and I can't wait to see you.

#YourFutureHusband

As a young boy, I would often imagine my very own wedding and the excitement of becoming a husband to the most beautiful woman on earth, my future wife. As I got older, I begin to explore the idea of what it would take for me to not only to be a future husband but how to be the best future husband I could be. My father exhibited the model of a good husband through his provision, faithfulness and vision toward my mother. Being faithful to her needs, listening to her heart and being a leader in the household. While this may seem like a simple task, it is often difficult due to the current trends of our modern society. A society where relationships and marriage have become a reality show for the followers of Instagram and Facebook, where status and popularity are valued more than the process of growing in unconditional love.

Sure, it is exciting to be recognized by the world of social media for our relationship aspirations but what about after the likes and comments of social media have ended, will that relationship stand the test of time or even the weight of commitment that marriage will require between two people. A romantic relationship between a man and woman must have a defined vision or else it will be swayed by the popularity of social media or the ever-changing opinions of individuals who do not have the best interest of the romantic relationship blossoming into a future marriage.

First let's define what marriage really means, marriage is an institution between a man and woman who have mutually pledged a lifetime commitment to each other.

Marriage is an institution that bring together two lives into one flesh, one spirit, and a clear vision. It is recognized as an act of social, legal and even spiritual unity as two people, the man and woman begin a lifetime mutual covenant with the full intention of connecting two diverse family lifelines to become the bridge to the next generation.

Marriage is also the establishment of two God-given purposes connecting together to illustrate the beauty of the fulfillment of true love.

Now, you may be asking yourself, how can I even begin this wonderful journey and even how can a romantic relationship blossom into that beautiful institution called marriage. It all begins with the man having a vision from God and the awareness that he must take responsibility for the woman he chooses to spend his life with.

The bible records in Proverbs 29:18, *"Where there is no vision, the people perish: but he that keepeth the law, happy is he."* It is the divine responsibility for the man to have a vision before his wife can arrive. When God gave Adam the responsibility to name the various plants and animals, Adam was walking out his purpose and that is when Eve was finally revealed. That's right, when a man is walking out his God-given purpose, it is inevitable that he will run into his good thing. Not his girlfriend, not a one night stand, not an option but his wife.

Just imagine a man so lost in his purpose that he just happens to find you in the process, you are his wife and he will not find you until he is found faithful putting God's purpose for his life in motion. For a woman is indeed a gift who was created by God to help the man carry his purpose as well as being highlighted with the responsibility of releasing from her womb the next generation of men and women who will build upon the legacy that is established between the husband and the wife.

The term wife has been loosely used in our society, it is no longer synonymous with the institution of marriage, but it is now equivalent to the idea of a long-term or seasonal girlfriend. However, the responsibility of a wife cannot be given to just any woman, she must be chosen by the right man. Not just any man but the man who first consulted the most important man in her life, her heavenly father.

Let me be the first to tell you, that her heavenly father is quite protective of the queen that she will become and she will be hidden or locked away until the right man is finally revealed. Even she will continue to be unhappy because the fullest of her value won't be realized until God sees fit to release her to her future husband.

A wife is a woman, whose body, mind and soul have been shaped for the lifetime journey with her husband. Believe it or not, who a woman ultimately marries depends on her level of maturity during each season of her life.

That is why it's very important, that before a woman begins taking steps toward a romantic relationship with a man that she examines the elements of what she desires in a man.

A woman's desire for a man should be shaped by pure intentions and motives. If status, popularity or convenience are in the mixture, then it is inevitable that over time she may grow tired during the romantic journey. She may then choose another man who fits the description of what she feels she needs for that season of her life but not the lifetime journey.

A woman's greatest desire is ultimately to be loved and love is indeed an action word. Love in its purest form requires hard work, consistent communication and faithfulness between two people.

Without these factors, love will be short-lived and subject to change based on feelings. It is very imperative for each man to have clear understanding that he cannot be wavering in his actions when it comes to the heart of a woman.

The heart of a woman was created to be loved and the love of her heart has the ability to carry many generations. A wife may one day become a mother or she may even be a mother already when she begins the marriage covenant. One of the most influential roles a woman will have is as a matriarch to the next generation.

Ladies, take out a pen and paper and ask yourself these questions, be honest with your answers because the questions are not often answered but just assumed based on the image of the culture.

1. What is my definition of a man?

2. Is he a man because he possesses, a six pack, six figures and a mansion?

3. Is he a man because he can afford you the most expensive gifts?

4. Does he have the vision to build the bridge for the next generation to walk on?

5. What is your definition of the term wife?

6. What is society's definition of the term wife?

7. Am I ultimately ready to be found by my future husband because of my beauty or because of the condition of my heart?

8. Am I healed from my past hurts?

9. Is My desire for a husband based on my desire to fulfill my purpose or because I'm tired of sleeping alone at night?

10. Am I ready for the responsibility that maintaining true love will require or am I just looking for the recognition of just having a romantic relationship?

 Ladies, these are few of the many questions, that you will need to ask yourself as you prepare for the future of becoming a wife.

#DearFuturewife,

This is only the beginning of great things to come between us, my whole life I've waited for this moment. As you patiently wait for me to arrive, know that your waiting is not in vain. You are everything I have imagined and so much more.

I love the way God created you to be, it's your smile, your hair and your personality that brings balance to my world.

Though you may have been disappointed, hurt and or heartbroken before this point, know that I made the choice to be with you no matter your past or your present because you're my future.

I look forward to raising our children, whether inherited or the ones we procreate.

To the family portraits we take, to the graduations where we hold hands and celebrate the accomplishments of our sons and daughters.

I'll be there for the better and I'll hold you during the worst.

Seasons may change, but my love for you will be forever

Arguments will come, but I can't wait to make up afterwards.

To the random dinner dates and movie nights. Our lifelines will come together to make a beautiful timeline that includes my arms around you cherishing the memories we will make after we say I do.

All this excitement has me ready to propose, but make sure you read further so you can enjoy this journey as much as I am here in the future

I love you and I'll see you soon.

#YourFutureHusband

#DearFuturewife, thank you for every prayer on my behalf

God shaped and molded me just for you, I won't take you for granted neither will I forget that you were heaven sent. My prayer has and always has been, Lord keep me in a position to hold her up because the job of a wife and mother takes the strength of a lifetime.

Our children already have the world's greatest mom!

#YourFutureHusband

As you prepare to read the chapters ahead, truly begin to examine your intent toward the institution of marriage. Marriage is indeed honorable and it must be entered into with the true understanding that it is not just an act, but it becomes a responsibility that both the man and woman must commit to fulfilling. There will be seasonal changes, life will happen but if the foundation is solid, then nothing can separate the future husband from you, his future wife

#DearFuturewife,

Are you ready for the journey that we will take together? I have chosen you as my bride and together we will accomplish many

things. I know we are two imperfect people coming together to perfect this lifetime journey together. We both will make mistakes, but I promise that I will be responsible for the vision that I am presenting before your eyes. Every heartbeat that you bring to my life transports the rhythm to the melody of my heart.

Together we harmonize our lives to created beautiful memories that we can replay to our future grandchildren. I will wait for you, I will not settle for just any woman. It's more than just make-up and curves. It's the color of your eyes, the shape of your hands and your unique DNA that God created as a perfect match for me. The first time you say hello, I'll know that your voice is the perfect harmony of my lifetime.

#YourFutureHusband

Exercise 1- What do you expect?

Write the characteristics that you desire your future husband to have, no matter what they may be.

Separate those characteristics from what is physical, emotional, spiritual, and natural.

Eliminate the physical characteristics and organize the other characteristics based on the order of importance for your future husband.

Compose a letter to your future husband, reveal to him only what you believe he should know about you.

Write a letter to your future husband telling him what to expect from you, be honest in the letter as you truly examine the person you are now and the person you desire to become.

Plan your dream wedding with a budget of 5,000, 7,500 and 9,000

Describe what you look forward to the most about marriage to your future husband.

What is your biggest fear about marriage?

After you answer these questions, reflect on the answers and proceed to chapter 2.

The Beautiful Future Wife

The many mornings that pass by as the questions are asked...... Why hasn't she been found?

To find an answer would take many stories to explore, phone calls, text messages and voice mails to maintain. Introduction after introduction, addition then subtraction multiplied by emotions and divided by distance and space that equates to moments of her storybook.

How much could it all be worth at the end of the day? Much more than you could imagine.

As time passes by, I am reminded of the many reasons why your beauty is timeless. When God created you, he smiled and said she will compliment many sons and fathers. When you walk, your strides harmonize with happily ever after.
Your eyes tell the story of your life experiences.
In your heart, lies the capacity to hold a generation together.

You're a future mom, a sister, a daughter, a wife and God's present to mankind.
Whether your 5"4, 5"7 or even 5"11, your ability to love is unlimited.

Your skin's tone are smooth moments that make every man look forward to a lifetime with you.

Even without make-up you bring excitement to the hearts of many men.

Whether your hair, is curly, natural or straight, the essence of who you are, goes beyond what is seen with the naked eye.

Your smile is a portrait of God's incredible creativity.
No matter your past, your name, height or weight, to that one man, you will be gorgeous forever.
You're the one made just for him and forever his love for you, will rewind.

Like the morning sunrise, every day you will rise.

Like the sunset, your reflection goes beyond what is seen in the mirror.

That's what makes you beautiful because every morning you wake up you'll be more beautiful to the future.

You're beautiful without restriction,

Like the blue skies ahead, you'll remain this way forever.

Chapter 2 - The Responsibility

#DearFutureWife

God has given me the enormous task of preparing my heart, mind and even my em

otions for your arrival. I will admit that along the way, I have faced many obstacles, one of which is how do I complete the vision God has given me, as well as preparing myself for a lifetime with you. As the man of your future household, it is important that you know I consider our future as very serious. When we finally meet, you will be the only woman in my life. I have put an end to any other possibilities and you're my choice. I look forward to seeing you very soon sweetheart,

#YourFutureHusband

Before a man chooses his wife, he must be void of wavering in his thoughts toward his destiny partner. He ultimately knows that his choice must intend to be final, not optional or a fantasy but knowing that in reality his season of singleness is ending. During a man's season of singleness, he begins to truly examine his thoughts toward women. He must begin to weigh the responsibility of sharing his life with not just any woman but the woman who will be his future wife.

The responsibility of a man choosing his wife is one that requires that he look beyond her outer beauty/physical appearance and examine if she measures up to the vision that God has called him to complete.

A man is visual in nature and his natural instincts can have the potential to lead him to make the wrong choice of who will be his future wife.

In a society, where outer beauty outweighs inner beauty, it is very important that each man truly understand that what he sees does not necessarily lead to what he will obtain in the future. The art of a man choosing his future wife can only be enhanced by his ability to see into her spirit. By viewing her spirit, he is able to go beyond her appearance and see her issues. Unfortunately, many women have mastered the art of concealing their issues, hurts, pains and hang-ups through make-up, curves, photo filters and trendy clothing. Often times it's the most beautiful women who are often misunderstood, hurting and hoping someone will listen.

How many times has she trusted men that only capitalized on her insecurity, leaving her hopeless to the reality that the man she thought chose her, really wanted her for just her physical features? Now with an emotional wall, she becomes numb to the possibility of being found by her future husband.

Each man that embarks upon the idea of choosing his future wife must be ready to handle the emotional elements that she will bring.

The emotional elements of a woman do not necessarily equate to drama, but it is her natural form of expression that she has inherited from birth.

Unfortunately, the emotional elements of a woman can be manipulated almost to a point where she will view a man based on his possessions but his character is left unmeasured. The character of a man is very important in his journey of choosing who his future wife will be. The bible records in Proverbs 20:6, *"that most will proclaim his own goodness but a faithful man who can find him."*

A man of integrity will choose the woman who has the ability to help him walk through the 4 seasons of his life and the 4 seasons of her life. The four seasons of life are the same as nature: Spring, Summer, Fall, and Winter. Before the man chooses his wife, he must value the choice of who his future wife will be. He must ask himself,

Can he handle her past?

Can he handle the idea of raising a child that is not biologically his?

Can he handle the many life changes that she will experience? *(Pregnancy, monthly cycle, motherhood)*

Will he remain faithful to her even in difficult times or times of misunderstanding?

Each woman will bring a unique emotional element that requires him to adjust, and this may even include preparing for fatherhood if his future wife already has children.

Just because a woman has children already, should not disqualify her from the possibility of becoming a future wife.

The responsibility of the man to choose the right woman is just as important as her understanding that marriage is not about the wedding, the carats of an engagement ring or the title of being a wife but the journey ahead requires hard work and patience from both the man and the woman.

Yes the man does choose her but she must be in position to be found, her position to be found is not determined by her outer beauty, her body type or skin tone but it is determined by her maturity to handle the strengths and weaknesses of the man who will be her husband.

The man God has for her may not be able to give her a 2 carat ring until 10 years later but has the character, faithfulness and consistent communication to handle all of the life changes that each of them will experience throughout their life journey.

The responsibility of the man choosing the right woman becomes easier when his thoughts toward her are shaped by pure motives and intentions. He cannot look for temporary pleasure or relief from a wife, but he must be ready to take ownership of the leadership that she will require in order for her to submit to his God-given vision.

When a woman chooses to submit to that man's vision, she is entrusting him to follow the purpose that God has set before his path and he is not selling her an unorganized dream.

The man must truly understand that presentation he makes to the woman he intends to spend his life must be authentic and pure. He is not only presenting her with his trust and his purpose, but he is also giving her a sneak preview of the type of leader he will be in the household.

The greatest compliment a man can give to his future wife is his consistent communication. Communication is the bridge between assumption of a matter and the actuality of a matter.

#DearFutureWife

I'm just a few more moments closer to your heart and I promise I am ready for whatever you bring to my world.

#YourFutureHusband

The GPS of a man's heart should be set toward a lifetime with his future wife, yes situations and circumstances will arise but God has given him the strength to carry, manage the gift of his future wife. His wife is the bonus that comes along with fulfilling his purpose. His future wife will have the necessary ingredients that will cultivate his gifts, talents and God-given abilities. When a man finds his future wife, he finds the rhythm of the song God has written for his destiny.

Once upon a season, there was a young man who desired to become a teacher. Throughout his college career, he dates a few young ladies but yet he found himself single going into his senior year of college. He then meets a wonderful young lady and his life begins to blossom, he receives a job right out of college and he then marries the young lady 2 years into his new career.

He then begin to experience sickness in his body and is temporarily out of work for a year. During this time, his wife is with him as he recovers from the illness never leaving his side and also working a full-time job so that the bills could be paid. The young man recovers from sickness and begins working as a teacher again, he now begins to tend to his wife as they are now expecting twin girls.

This is an example of many of the situations that can likely occur when life happens, however, when both the man and woman understand the responsibility of maintaining their covenant of marriage, they will survive through even the toughest season.

Unfortunately, this responsibility is not emphasized in our modern society as the focus is living in the moment but the longevity of the journey is left unmeasured. Life will bring many changes but when both the man and women take responsibility for the building of true love, then the goal of future marriage will be reached.

Exercise 2

Ladies,

If you are currently in a relationship, ask yourself is this person I am currently with the person I see myself with for a lifetime? Or is this just a person for the moment?

If you are currently single, ask yourself can I truly be trusted with the strengths and weakness of my future husband?

If not why?

Carefully answer these question and then begin to read Chapter 3.

Chapter 3 - The Commitment

#DearFutureWife,

 From the moment we meet until my last breath I won't let you go. There so much I can't wait to share with you, I promise that this journey will be memorable.

#YourFutureHusband

Imagine the excitement, the day has finally come. The man has finally chosen his bride and now the clock starts ticking toward the wedding. The thoughts of the moment he proposes, the joy of choosing the perfect wedding dress. The design of the wedding invitations and the reception guest list but here comes the next question?

Does he truly understand that once he has chosen his future wife, he has transitioned from the idea of her to her now being the priority woman in his life?

When the man considers the possibility of choosing the woman he intends on spending his life with, his focus must now shift toward long-term and he must reject the idea of her being temporary. Of course, there will be many things, circumstances, and even people that will be seasonal but who he intends to be his wife must be a choice that he will commit a lifetime too. The man must consider, that her heart desires to be loved eternally.

He must avoid having a sense of entitlement toward women, even a good man must prepare himself for the weight of commitment that it takes to have a life with his future wife.

Though the influence of society will be strong, he must establish that his choice will be well thought out and represent longevity toward his future wife. A man's commitment must be shaped for the enormous responsibility of having a wife and also a family

The maximum requirement for a woman should be consistent commitment. Her requirements toward marriage must be geared toward the intangible quality of unconditional commitment. Though it is common that each woman has to be showered with gifts, love and affection, she will be left searching for emotional fulfillment without consistent commitment.

Because women are naturally emotional, the depth of her love for that man is strengthened when there is a strong level of consistent commitment from that man. No matter how much money may be spent on her, her desire will be fulfilled through intangibles that have no monetary cost but by, what is more, valuable than money.

When a man chooses his future wife, his commitment to her must match the words he speaks. The value of a man's word decrease when the strength of his commitment is less equivalent to his words toward her.

A woman's initial view of security is established through commitment, emotional stability and consistent communication from a man. Her view of security cannot be based on a man's wealth, status or possessions. If her view of security is based on the material elements, then she may choose a man who will provide her heart with a lesser value than she was created to have.

The GPS of a woman's heart should be set toward the destination of a lifetime with her future husband, but if it is set toward temporary elements such as what a man has in that particular season of his life then she is most likely not mature enough to handle the value of being a future wife. Her thoughts of being a wife must not end with the wedding ceremony, her mind must be prepared to handle the journey that she will take with her future husband.

She must realize that the wedding is indeed one single day, but the marriage is for a lifetime. While there is excitement after the start of the engagement process, this is only the beginning of the marathon know as marriage. Though the wedding day is deemed important, it can easily become the primary focus and the seriousness of marriage is neglected.

When a woman becomes a wife, her emotions become heighten because she is submitting her heart to her husband. This is why a man must carefully examine the woman he intends to spend his life with and the emotional investment that she requires from him.

The man has a responsibility to provide the woman with love and affection as well as emotional stability. Contrary to popular belief, the size of the engagement ring that a man gives to a woman he has chosen to be his future wife is not a measure of his love for her. The engagement ring is symbolic of his intention of a lifetime commitment to her and also what he is able to purchase within his personal budget. The engagement ring is not a measure of the depth of his love for his future wife because his love for her will be unconditional.

Unconditional love cannot be measured in monetary value but can only be measured by consistency, loyalty, honesty and unselfishness. Unconditional love must be exhibited by both the man and woman and this can be displayed through their mutual commitment to each other.

Commitment is an action that promotes the intention of being successful in a particular area. Before the man chooses his wife, he must prepare to master the principle of commitment. The man must be committed to carrying out his God-given vision. Once he begins his commitment to his purpose, then he will choose the woman that best fits the mold of his destiny.

His choice must not be determined by the trend of the culture but by the increasing value of the legacy he intends to build with his future wife. He must truly understand that the woman he chooses must be able to manage the changes he will experience throughout his life as well as him being able to manage the changes she will experience.

#DearFutureWife,

I cannot promise that every day will be perfect but I do promise that I am committed to what the future holds for you and I. I'm not afraid to love you, the good, the bad and even the most painful parts of you. My heart is committed to the reality of you as my wife.

Unfortunately, due to the current trend of our modern culture, commitment is of lesser value and not even considered a necessary quality in romantic relationships. Many women have adopted the idea of love and marriage equal to the value of a man's current financial status, his possessions, his status and even his style of clothing.

However, a man must first be measured by the development of his intangible qualities.

Can he be trusted with your heart?

Will he walk with you through difficult seasons of your life?

Will he be honest with you?

Will he communicate consistently with you?

Each Man may ask these questions

Will she walk with me even if I am faced with a season of financial strain?

Will she respect me as a man?

A man's ultimate desire is to be respected by his future wife and if he feels that the respect that he desires will not be provided by that woman then he most likely consider another choice for his future wife. When a man chooses his bride, he must put an end to the idea of her being an option or a choice of convenience. Her beauty will fade, the make-up will be removed, but the pureness of her heart will determine if she is ultimately chosen as his bride.

Commitment is an intangible element that is only developed through the understanding that unconditional loyalty must be developed before unconditional love is birthed. Each man must consider if he is ready to commit to loving the woman who he will choose as his future wife. Each woman must consider that though she is chosen, is she ready to commit to the good, the bad and the ugly of the journey ahead with her future husband.

The commitment that is displayed by the man is as equally important as the commitment that is displayed by the woman. The man and woman must be committed to the common goal of providing each other with the intangible elements that will build the strength of their future marriage, set the direction of their future marriage and establish an unbroken bond between that man and that woman. Commitment is the heartbeat of a romantic relationship and it is the foundation of a future marriage. Without commitment, the possibility of a romantic relationship blossoming into a future marriage will be more of a fantasy but not a strong possibility.

Exercise 3- Intangible Elements

Choose the 3 Intangible elements that you desire your future husband to have.

1. Loyal

2. Honesty

3. Commitment

4. Faithfulness

5. Consistency

6. Accountability

7. Trust

8. Communication

9. Compassion

10. Understanding

After choosing the 3 intangible elements that desire your future to have, rate the intangible elements by importance in your future romantic relationship or if you are currently in a relationship ask yourself if these elements truly in your relationship.

Once you have completed this exercise proceed to read Chapter 4

Chapter 4- The Connection

#DearFutureWife,

 I knew the moment we met that we were an instant match. I truly believe in my heart that our love will pass the test of time. I miss you already even though we haven't met, talk to you soon

#YourFutureHusband

The gift of life provides each of us with memories we will never forget, many will even say that finding true love is a moment that is often unforgettable. But once true love is discovered how can it be maintained long-term? Can true love be sustained by feelings alone or is there more that must be explored?

Let's first examine the definition of true love. True love is defined as the honest commitment that is birthed from the pure intentions of an individual's desire to bring genuine happiness to another person through the consistency of actions that add value to the intangible elements that cultivate unconditional love.

Before true love is reached there must be a commitment to maintaining the actions that cultivate unconditional love. Before true love can be fully birthed, there must be a commitment to building mutual love between the man and the woman. When a man is considering who he will spend his life with, he considers the cost of building and sustaining the love that will allow her heart to rest in the future reality of being his wife.

When a woman is chosen by the man who will be her future husband, she has counted the cost of the journey that she will embark upon with that man.

Contrary to popular belief, being in love is not based on feeling alone, it is also a choice to continue the exploration of the process to reach the desired destination of those same feelings being reciprocated in return. The basis of being in love with another individual varies and it is often difficult to measure the depth of a person's romantic feelings because the shelf life of each individual's romantic feelings may vary based on past experiences, current expectations, cultural influence and maturity.

The romantic connection between the man and woman should be shaped toward the idea of the life journey known as marriage. The woman has been strategically shaped by God to handle the purpose and destiny that will come with her future husband's destiny and she also has been blessed with the ability to touch his heart like no other woman can.

The most important intangible element of building true love is trust between that man and that woman. Trust is an action that eliminates the idea of fear becoming the driving force for a growing romantic relationship. However, many individuals may choose a person who may fit the convenience of the present time or based on past pain/heartbreak.

While the feeling of finding true love is indeed very fulfilling experience, true love cannot be measured by the constraints of time.

There is no classification of time when an individual may show evidence of being in love with another individual but the origin of that love must be connected to pure motives or else the flame known as love will eventually burn out.

Trust is the bridge that connects two hearts to the commitment necessary to maintain a lifetime of love, trust is a two-way street that requires time, patience and the endurance of the seasonal changes that life will bring.

When God created man, he gave him the blueprint of truly loving a woman and that begins when he is walking in his God-given purpose.

When a man begins walking out his God-given purpose, the vision that is over his life sends out a connection signal to the heart of his future wife. The connection signal of a man's purpose may attract many women, but he will choose the woman who best fits the mold of his destiny. The man is responsible for making the initial introduction to the woman who he believes best fits his purpose but it is ultimately the woman's choice to decide if she is willing to walk with him as his destiny unfolds, as well as knowing if her destiny will match with his future.

A man's future wife will either be already in position to handle his destiny or she will choose to become a part of his destiny and begin the adjustment process of building the true love necessary to cultivate a lifetime with her future husband. The romantic connection between the man and woman cannot be sustained through feelings and emotions alone, each of them must truly understand that building true love is a journey, not a moment

It is the responsibility of both the man and woman to maintain the connection that will cultivate a long-lasting love between them. Because women are emotional, her connection to loving a man is strengthened through time, communication, affection, and faithfulness. Because men are visual, his connection to loving a woman is strengthened through honesty, loyalty, and consistency.

The connection of true love cannot be based on material elements, convenience or shallow view of love. Being in love with the idea of love will most certainly fall short of producing true love between a man and woman, love is a journey and it is only maintained through intangible elements that can neither be created or copied but replicated through time, experience and the observation of true love exhibited by those who have successfully cultivated true love in a romantic relationship with the opposite sex.

The journey of true love will differ for each individual but will ultimately lead to pure love being birthed between a man and a woman. While affection is a very important element in the process of building true love, even affection alone cannot sustain the connection between the man and woman in a romantic relationship. Affection in its purest form is the combination of accrued consistency combined with a strong commitment and cannot be based on the temporal pleasure of a few solitary moments.

It is very important that when a man is considering his future bride that he has the vision to see beyond her physical appearance and truly see the depth of her heart. The heart of a woman desires true love from a man and a man's love for her cannot be based on the physical benefits she may possess but his love for her must be connected to the desire to fulfill God's beautiful promise of marriage. True love, when it is birthed, has the ability to live on even to the next generation.

However, due to the cultural and social influences of our modern society, the image of a woman has been reduced an ideal size, shape and status. But when a man has a vision for his life he will choose his future wife based on the blueprint of his destiny not the influence of the culture. Whether she is 5'5, 5'10 or even a little overweight, he will choose to love her no matter what seasons she will experience in the future. He is committed to being by her side through sickness, good and bad health, her successes and even her failures. Her future will also be committed to his future no matter how much of his God-given vision is completed because her love will cultivate the ingredients that will help him complete the vision of his life. When a man chooses his future wife, he is also prepared to release his pride and walk with her. When a woman is chosen by her future husband, she makes the choice to love him just as he will also love her.

Each woman's heart is likened unto the blueprint of a house, it is unique but has specific measurements that cannot be easily reached until it is in the hands of the right architect (her future husband).While the process of building true love between the man and woman is necessary for the longevity of true love, the connection is vital to the health of pure love being exhibited in a romantic relationship. Each man must wisely choose his bride, a woman is worth more than a one night stand or just a moment of random time.

A woman's heart is her most valued asset and her ability to love is so strong that it even lives beyond the grave through her children. Each woman must understand that being a wife is not about what she can gain in the future but what she will build with her future husband is an unbreakable bond that God will honor.

Chapter 5- The Stories

#DearFutureWife,

 Let's make this a walk to remember. My hand and your hand forever connected to the bright future ahead of us.

I love you

#YourFutureHusband

One Moment later

 Anticipating the moment that was right before his eyes, a heart that begin to explore the idea of forever, his footsteps now measured the excitement that was ahead.

The clock ticks as his palms are now sweaty, the story of this night was yet to be written.

Not to mention, phone calls and text messages of well wishes that made him even more nervous.

The clock now reads midnight as a new horizon begins, the sound of nervousness harmonized with the open elevator door as he walked in, 5 floors until the moment of a lifetime was to occur, the stage is now set as all the witnesses were in place for history in the making.

The camera starts as the spotlight now shifts to the countdown of seconds. Two knocks later, the door knob clicks. It was now or never for this chapter. With hands in his pocket, he walks over to the side of the bed where she laid and begin to speak.

"From the moment you walked into my life, I knew you were more than special. I now see that my life would be incomplete without you. For better or worse, I will always be here with you. I only have one question to ask you, sweetheart. With this ring will you be wife?"

A diamond ring, symbolic of two unique paths uniting forever. She was speechless, but something was still missing.

The rooms were now quiet as everyone in the room awaited her answer. He leans forward to embrace her, but she pulls away. Her expression is a straight face. He again asks, "Baby will you marry me?" She nodded with a soft yes.

He puts the ring on her finger as they both walked into the hallway. With anger in her voice, she spoke the words "This is not the ring I desire, and why are you proposing when you know you're not ready?"

He replied "I love you and I want to spend the rest of my life with you, I believe this is the start of a new journey forever."

She replied "You're not ready to marry me."

His eyes begin to water as the clock read 10PM and they both walked back in the house.

The truth is that what was supposed to be a wonderful occasion was now a nightmare.

No ring, no wedding, just questions left unanswered.

All there was to remember was the look on her face and the cold syllables she spoke to him in the most awaited moment.

365 days pass by still no wedding, but one broken heart triggered by the right ring at the wrong time.

Past Due Notice

Birthdays, anniversaries and many smiles. Quickly, I turned into a gentleman and accepted the role.

Butterflies begin to overtake my stomach as my mind begin to run in circles. I started first and she followed. This was not a usual friendship.

She was given access to all my deepest secrets. And I begin to let the real me show flaws and all.

She was worth it. This was my soul mate and I wasn't going to let her go. I had a renewed sense of hope knowing that the time would come.

She was my best friend because of the secrets that were shared. An attraction that matured into an unconditional love for her.

So inspired that I begin praying to God saying thank you I now have hope for a future with her. The letters begin to be written. Then the day came when I received a text message, asking me the question of when we could soon go out.

I became excited and begin to plan. I made up in her mind that I was going to do something I never done. I wanted more than friendship. I was ready to take the next step and be with her exclusively.

Unfortunately, because I waited too long, this wonderful blessing was now just my imagination. I replayed the images of a dream that wouldn't come true because I was too busy being the opposite of the man she fell in love with.

My fantasy is an enemy of my reality, I missed out on the quality search for the perfected TV woman with no substance but only commercial entertainment.

A hard goodbye as I change the channel yet again.

True Love

They started out as friends, but this quickly progressed to something more than imagined. She was a woman of much purpose and a smile that gave you sunshine in the midst of rainy days.

Many hours spent in the arms of each other as they both prayed for guidance for the future.

A great relationship was in motion and the future appeared bright. Then a simple disagreement brought the reality of the differences between them.

He was a high school drop-out and she was an RN. He spent long hours cleaning bathrooms after school while she gave medicine to the elderly Monday through Friday.

To others, they appeared to be incompatible but to each other it wasn't hard to notice that an unbreakable connection was building.

Then tragedy would hit like none other, she would lose her mother and sister 1 month apart.

2 funerals, 2 memories but no one but him to comfort her during the lonely times she has at work.

Phone calls text messages they would share as he would wake up out of his sleep to break her lunch to her overnight shift.

You see she was used to being showered with gifts by many men, but mentally she just wanted to know that someone would always be there.

Not only was he there but he was consistent with his efforts.

However, he looks nothing like she is used too. She begins to ignore his efforts in hopes of getting a man who was much more established.

Missed phone calls and text message from him, she is now in the arms of another man.

Devastated he begins the process of moving on as he knows he must focus on himself.

He earns his high school diploma and begins working for a grocery store.

7 Years later, he becomes a supervisor. She is now a single mother struggling to pay bills because she was promised that she would be taken well care of so she stopped working as a nurse and because a housewife.

While shopping she runs into the guy she once knew, not only has he matured but he is now preparing to move to another city for a higher paying position as a store manager.

He hugs her and wishes her well, knowing that though he loved her their season has passed by.

She regrets letting him go but he is happy because he is free to love without restriction.

Never underestimate the initial beginning of where love begins, it's not about the image, it's about the foundation.

When love is based on the inner value and not the outer wealth, it will cultivate a love story that won't end up like this.

Closure

Looking into the last time I wrote for last time to define the moments of the time period I'm about to describe.

Many nights defined by words never spoken and thoughts never uttered.

The clock read 10:47 as my world was introduced to the infamous phrase I'm ready to move on without you.

Quickly the questions of why, why, why are answered with a goodbye through the introduction of her new relationship via the World Wide Web.

The momentum was in my favor because according to opinions of the masses I wasn't man enough to handle what you had to over.

The reality was evident that you chose the man who was best for your view of the American Dream.

Maybe I just wanted a better future for what we could have been.

But either way your love for me had reached its climax as you became engaged shortly thereafter and I was left to wonder about the future ahead.

That's when dividends of shoulda', coulda', and woulda' all made sense as I chose to use this experience as a reminder that some doors have to close in order for you to fly higher.

The window to my soul became clear as I embraced the brightness of my future ahead.

No forgiveness is necessary, just a memory that I use as inspiration for others who will cross my path.

Chapter 6- The Memories

#DearFutureWife,

I will never forget the moment you smiled for the first time, I knew right then I would be willing to do whatever it takes to make you smile again.

#YourFutureHusband

Often, we are introduced to the view of memorable events such as weddings, marriage proposals through various avenues such as romantic movies, social media and we may even witness the birth of a child. But the origins of those moments we never forget, are birthed from memories that may seem small but begin the pathway for greater moments to occur in the future. Many times a simple phone call from the significant other is misplaced and the focus on the moment of the marriage proposal is weighted more heavily.

Life is filled with many possibilities that are left unfulfilled because simple moments are misplaced in the pursuit of the image of a memory that has yet been experienced but is expected to occur.

If the question were asked of many women about their expected reaction to a marriage proposal by their current significant other or the significant other they plan to have in the future.

Most women would reply that the marriage proposal would be the moment they most looked forward to because it was previously presented as the beginning of future wedding plans and the expectations of compliments along with well wishes.

But what if the bridge of those most intimate moments such as a marriage proposal, or the wedding ceremony was based on the expectations of others, but the road to true fulfillment in a romantic relationship is left unpaved.

It is the unseen memories shared privately between that man and that woman that strengthen the validity of the unforgettable moments that will be evident to others. Such as the good morning texts from her, the dinner invitations from him, the holding of each other's hands, the unseen prayers for one another and the moments of unspoken words with positive thoughts.

While this may seem very small to many, it is these simple elements that transform possibilities into reality and strengthen the idea of forever between that man and that woman.

Before the element of these wonderful possibilities can be birthed, each must set in his mind who he desires to share those moments with, he must set his focus on the effort to commit to the who he will ultimately choose.

The man must place his thoughts in the idea of choosing the right woman, he must reject the idea of having other women as options or backup plans.

If a man is unsure about the idea of a particular woman in his life, he must be honest with that woman so that she can be in position to be found by another man who will seriously choose her as his future wife. If he is unsure due to him considering more than one woman, then it is best that he remain single.

The value of a woman was defined by God himself. In God's eyes, she is identified as a daughter, a wife, a mother and matriarch to the next generation. The woman should not be viewed as a mistress or sexual object because these titles are associated with a woman who is valued much lower than the value that the heavenly father has placed on her from birth.

When a man finds his future wife, he will introduce her to the origin of memories that will cultivate her ability to love him and will build the bridge of unconditional love between that man and that woman. The journey of true love is a walk of faith, not a leap, it is a culmination of simple memories that build the moments of true love. The journey of true love is not defined by the moments that most recognized such as the wedding or the marriage proposal, but it is the memories that were made beforehand.

A moment is defined as a particular time or stage marked by a series of prior events or memories leading up to that specific time. A memory is defined as the act of recalling events, impressions or the recollection of previous times that give birth to the anticipation for an expected outcome. When true love is in motion, the heart becomes the camera as it photographs the special memories of the journey ahead. The marriage proposal is a single event, the wedding is one single day but it's the memories that were created along the journey were the depth of true love is defined.

The memories of true love between a man and a woman are birthed when there is a mutual commitment between them.

Without the simple memories of romance between a man and a woman, there is a possibility that there will be more focus placed on single events that are associated with true love but lack the substance to maintain un-unconditional love long term. Love is not a single moment or a single day, but it is a journey of moments that build the bridge of eternal commitment between that man and that woman. If love is defined as a single moment or just one single day, then its significance will be subject to the ever-changing circumstances that life brings.

It's the memories such as the first initial meeting, that first text message, the sound of her voice early in the morning or even the smell of the perfume on the first date.

It's the look on her face when she realizes, she just spilled coffee on his shirt or even how she looks early in the morning before make-up is applied or her hair is in place. The memories that are created during the journey of true love between the man and the woman are essential to the growth of their unconditional love.

For Each Other

It's the smiles on her face and the confidence in his ability to provide her with the emotional security that she desires in her heart that will solidify her saying yes to the future marriage proposal.

Her acceptance of the marriage proposal will not be based on social or financial gain, but her acceptance of the marriage proposal will be based on the foundation of beautiful memories that were built from the beginning.

The man's proposal to his future wife will not be based on the obligation to fulfill standards set by family and friends but it will originate from his desire to provide her with the love she truly desires from him and his commitment to walking with her through the future seasons of her life.

Before either the man or woman reach the point of being prepared for the future occasions such as the marriage proposal or the wedding ceremony, they must value each memory that is created during the journey of true love.

During the journey of true love, the good will outweigh the bad and the unique differences between that man and that woman will actually draw them closer to each other.

The key to the woman's heart does not lie in the possessions she will gain from that man, but it is the love that opens her heart to the reality of true love.

The keys to a man's heart lie not in the beauty of a woman's appearance but in her ability to grow with him as his purpose evolves. As the memories between the man and the woman continue to build, true love will naturally take its course, time will strengthen the connection between them and happily ever after goes from pure imagination to pure reality.

#DearFutureWife, *My search is now complete. The moment our eyes connected, the GPS of my heart said destination reached. I Love you*

#YourFutureHusband

Chapter 7- The Promise

#DearFutureWife,

There will be good times and there will be times where life isn't as pleasant as we hope it to be but the vision that we are building will never change. No matter what season may come, I am committed to the completion of a lifetime with you.

True Love is not a perfect journey, in fact, it is two flawed individuals coming together to produce the beautiful portrait of true love. Many people start upon the journey of true love but due to the uncertainties of life, they give up along the way due to circumstances that can neither be explained nor calculated.

It must be truly understood that in life there are few to almost no guarantees, the only consistent factors are birth and death. Though the sacred institution of marriage is a promise, it is a promise that many have failed to fulfill.

A promise is defined as a declaration of something that can either be completed or the declaration of fulfilling a prior expected result given to another individual.

A promise is also subject to the possibility that it may be broken, adjusted or even forgotten by the person who made the promise.

This can also be applied to the journey of building true love because the ultimate promise of marriage is not completed until death. To most individuals, relationships and marriage are related to the understanding that certain expectations are going to be fulfilled by that individual.

A promise is the expectation of something to be completed in the future.

Here's a better explanation, marriage is a promise of walking until death, not until a person's expectations are ultimately met. The journey of true love will involve two individuals from diverse backgrounds, whether it's two different nationalities, races or even two income levels. True love between the man and the woman is the beginning of the journey toward the promise of marriage.

During each season, an individual's expectation will vary but this will change when an individual begins the journey of true love.

Their expectations must shift toward what is best for both that man and woman as they collectively walk together in true love. Knowing that the journey of true love is one that requires patience and time, it is best that each man and woman truly examine their intentions and to why they desire true love. True love is not a feeling or a moment, it is a lesson that will be constantly learned as two individuals, draw closer together.

True love is a daily decision that requires a consistent commitment of two people. Even the journey of true love has few guarantees, there are no guarantees of perfection and true love is a process that can only be built with time.

However, true love does guarantee that two people will grow in love and will learn the true meaning of love.

During the journey of true love, both individuals will develop the intangible elements to maintain the love that is necessary to begin, maintain and complete the promise of marriage.

Once upon a time there was a young man named David. He came from a humble background. He watched both of his parents struggle to make ends meet and as he got older he begin to handle the chores as he watched his mother become sick and unable to take care of herself.

David graduated from high school and left home to attend college, determined to make his mother and father proud. During his junior year, David meets a young lady named Jessica. Jessica was considerably attractive and had just gotten out of a relationship when she met David.

Despite his interest in Jessica, David was focused on finishing his degree while

Jessica was hoping for things to take off between her in David. David and Jessica began a friendship, but soon Jessica began dating a man who seemed to be focused on her more than David was. A year passed by and David graduated from college while Jessica became engaged to another young man named Benjamin. Benjamin was a retail banker and was established in his career, Jessica saw Benjamin as a man who could provide for her in their future marriage. He proposed to her with a 1.5 carat ring and Jessica begin to plan for her wedding, David begins medical school and Jessica marries Benjamin.

5 years pass by and David is 2 years into his residency program while Jessica seems happily married. One day Jessica comes home early from work to find Benjamin kissing another woman on the couch.

Jessica storms out of the house in an outrage and a few minutes later she is involved in a head-on collision. She is knocked unconscious and is paralyzed from the waist down. Benjamin then visits

71

Jessica in the hospital bed and serves her divorces papers as she lies in her bed wondering if she will regain the ability to walk again.

Jessica begins rehab and ironically runs into David during one of her physical therapy sessions, she begin to cry as David consoles her concerning the end of her marriage to Benjamin.

Though the opportunity has presented itself for David and Jessica, to explore the possibility of a future together, they both agree that each of them must move forward in their lives as just friends.

The promise of marriage is all inclusive of the good and bad, and will follow along in the journey of the two people, striving to grow in true love. Though marriage is a promise, the fulfillment of true love in marriage is worth a lifetime.

True love is indeed a story that is likely unscripted, yet it is a blessing to all those who experience it and a lesson to all those who are willing to learn during the journey of growing in love.

Ask yourself........

Am I ready for the sacrifice of the promise known as marriage?

Am I ready to truly build the true love that leads to marriage?

If your answer is yes, then know that you are dressing your heart for the journey?

If your answer is no, ask yourself how do I prepare for the sacrifice true love will entail?

#DearFutureWife,

My prayers have been answered. You walked into my life and now my heart has begun to count the seconds until we are together forever.

Activity

Define the promise of marriage.

What are your expectations of the promise of marriage?

Do you believe the promise of marriage is one that is broken quite often in our culture?

#DearFutureWife

I promise that my heart won't be given to anyone else but you. I waited my whole life for this moment and I will not let it pass me by.

I love you

#Your Future Husband

Chapter 8 - The Prayers

#Dear Future Wife,

Every day I pray that I am prepared for your arrival. That my heart has no residue of past hurts but that I can freely give you the keys to the door to my future with you forever.

#YourFutureHusband

Prayer for her Heart

Father in Jesus Name,

I pray for the heart of this woman who one day will be the future wife of the man you have set aside for her destiny. Protect her emotions from the damages of the past hurts, pains and even the misunderstood situations. *She was created by you Lord to love her future husband for a lifetime and she is a gift for his destiny. She is not only special, but she has been molded by you to walk with her future husband in every season of his life. Prepare her for the task of learning how to love her future husband. Let every desire of her heart be fulfilled as she grows into the woman that you have destined her to be.*

In Jesus Name

Prayer for her Health

Father in Jesus name, I pray for the health of my future wife.

Give her wisdom to know how to take care of her body, protect her from disease, mental illness, and emotional breakdowns. Bless her each morning to wake up with a clear mind and heart to live a healthy fulfilling life with her future husband.

In Jesus name

Prayer for her Vision

Father in Jesus name, I pray for the direction of this future wife. Let her eyes be opened about her true purpose in life, that she will not be just another woman who fits the mold and description of the current trend of the culture but that she will create a beautiful legacy that will bless many future generations. Direct her steps to the best career path and even give her wisdom to manage all resources you put in her hand so that she will produce the wealth that comes from her full purpose.

In Jesus Name Amen

Prayer for her Emotions

Father in Jesus name,

I pray for the emotional health of this virtuous future wife. Let her know even now that no matter what her past may be, that her future is brighter than it ever has been before. I pray that every disappointment, heartbreak will be the bridge to lead her to be the best future wife that she can be. That the love she will give will not be based on what she will gain but it will be based on truth and purity toward her future husband. That she will be free to love and not walk in fear of true love.

In Jesus Name

Prayer for Her Patience

Thank you, Lord Jesus, for building the patience of this future wife. Give her the wisdom to reject anything that is less than what you've promised her regarding her future husband. That she will not accept the norms of the modern culture but that she will wait for the man that matches the mold of her destiny as a future wife. That her waiting is not in vain but that she is being perfected as a beautiful portrait of virtue toward her future husband. Surround her with wise counsel, so that she will be prepared for the journey of true love that is ahead of her

In Jesus name

Prayer for Gifts

I thank you for this future wife that you placed on this earth to fulfill a purpose. She will not only accomplish great things, but she will also influence others to follow their God-given purpose. She will not look to emulate any other woman, but she will stand out because she will know her unique purpose in life. She is a compliment to her future husband and a gift to those connected to her.

In Jesus Name

Before a man makes any promises, writes the vision or even chooses his future wife, he must first pray so that his decision can be directed in the right path. Because of the magnitude of marriage, the man must choose his future wife wisely.

The choice of his future wife must be one that he intends to live with and he must base his choice on her worth, not her outer appearance. His choice must be shaped according to his God-given purpose and this

79

can only be revealed through that man's relationship with his heavenly father. As a man gets closer to his heavenly father, he receives access to the combination lock of his future wife's heart.

The combination lock of a man's future wife is not in her beauty, her possessions, but it lies in the pureness of her heart and how it divinely shifts to adjust to that man's vision. Just as a woman's heart adjusts to a man's vision, his heart will also adjust to her vision and together their visions will create a beautiful portrait of two collective purposes growing in true love.

Though it is very easy to follow the current trend of relationships in our modern day culture, each man and woman must truly evaluate their motivation for the desire of entering into the institution of marriage.

It is through prayer that each individual is able to view their heart from a pure perspective. It's through the eyes of our heavenly father that we are truly able to prepare our hearts our minds and even our spirit for the journey of growing in true love.

The bible says in Jeremiah 17:9 that our hearts are deceitfully wicked above all things and desperately wicked who can know it.

Naturally our hearts are flawed and if we are not directed by our heavenly Father, then we are capable of even deceiving ourselves that we have found true love when we may have just found relief for the moment. God is the ultimate example of true love despite our flaws, he still loves each of us unconditionally.

The journey of true love begins with the prayer of a man who desires to be connected to not just any woman but his future wife. The question I now ask to you as a future wife, Are you worth the journey? Are you worth the responsibility?

Can you handle the seasons that will come along with being a wife?

DearFutureWife

Are you ready? I know that a lifetime with you is something I look forward to.

I love you

#YourFutureHusband

Chapter 9 - True Love Forever

#DearFutureWife.

I am so excited about the journey that we are about to embark upon together. Hopefully, you've enjoyed this wonderful letter I've written for you thus far.

As I stand here in the future, I smile knowing that I will have the pleasure of calling you my wife. I am committed to the task of doing everything it takes to love you.

You may even ask yourself later in life, Why Did I choose you?

I chose you because you were the missing link to the fullness of my purpose being fulfilled, even with my future success I desire to share it will you.

This morning I asked God to watch over you until we meet and I know that you will be one of the greatest blessings I will receive in my life.

I love you, #YourFutureHusband

True love is indeed a beautiful thing, it was never meant to last for just a moment or just a season but the duration of a lifetime. A lifetime of two lifelines defined by commitment, responsibility and a solid foundation of consistency between the man and woman.

During this life, there will be a strong connection, countless memories and stories that will inspire many. It will all begin with the many prayers that will be prayed by him as he understands the promise he will fulfill just as she will fulfill that promise also.

Ultimately it will take two decisions to begin the journey of true love, the man makes the decision to pursue the woman he desires to grow closer and she mutually chooses the presentation that is placed before her eyes. The man must make a true choice on who he intends to spend his life with, the woman must choose the man who she know will cultivate her desire to be loved.

The right man will protect her heart, her emotions and will build the unbreakable bond that will secure the future of growing unconditional love between that man and that woman. As stated by a wonderful friend of mine, *"Home is where the heart is."* When she smiles, he knows that her heart has opened its door.

True love, is knowing that when man and woman will choose each other every day, no matter what each day will bring. Yes, he will be presented with various choices, situations, and even another beautiful woman will come across his path but each day he will choose the same woman he chose the day before and that is you. Yes, you are amazing and there will be many men who will make their presentation to you with various gifts, but the right man will have the character that is more valuable than anything money can buy.

You are not just any woman, you are special and right man has everything that will cultivate you becoming the best woman you can be.

Your past is not a factor, your future will be better than you expect because right now you are becoming the woman that will put the biggest smile on his face. Yes, you have the ability to make any man smile but the right man will love you despite your flaws.

Whether it's early in the morning when the make-up is off or even a simple Thursday after a hard day's work, he is committed to her no matter what.

You're not just a typical girlfriend, you're a future wife, your heart is his home, and your heartbeat is the doorbell that rings each time he is near you. He will not choose you because of your looks, your weight or your status but he will choose you because he knows that you will provide him with the love he desires and he will love you with the passion that you desire from your future husband.

You're a queen that was created by God to make history on earth, you will be his story that will be remembered and recited by future generations.

You may be reading this book with a broken heart or you may be afraid of looking in the mirror and embracing the beauty God gave, but true love is closer than you think.

True love will come your way when you least expect it but when it shows up, will you be ready? It's nothing like you've seen on television and movies.

You'll know without question that you've laid your eyes on the man whom you will call your future husband. He will choose you and you will choose him, he will even be a great father to your kids, even if he is not the biological father. Just because you are a mother doesn't disqualify you from true love, God is just preparing you for his best.

Let's begin a new trend in your life, starting now just imagine being in the arms of the man who truly loves you. He's not looking at the fact that you've been divorced or even looking at your past mistakes, he just wants the chance to love you.

This man knows that as soon as he meets you, he will begin preparing his mind for the reality of forever with you. Being his future wife goes far beyond just a title, you will have the most amazing task of providing comfort, joy, and care for the man you will call your future husband.

In a world where social media paints the image of what relationships appear to be, there will be true love behind the scenes as you become the woman that best fits the mold of his dream come true. The words, *'I love you'* won't be cliché or just a phrase to manipulate you, but they will be words that are pure and true. As you've read this book, my hope is that you've been inspired to become the best future wife to your future husband.

Don't just prepare for the wedding but know your journey starts now.

Though many women anticipate the day of receiving the engagement ring, remember the ring is indeed a symbol of the huge responsibility that you will carry as a future wife.

Yes, it is exciting, many people will wish you well through social media, calls and text messages but the real journey begins well before the engagement. Commit to being the woman who stands out from the trend of the culture.

The woman who preserves her body for marriage, the woman who will cherish the journey of true love and not just the image of true love. True love is a journey that is reserved for the man and the woman who are willing to use the intangible elements to cultivate true love. Which journey will you choose? Will you choose the road that puts more emphasis on possessions rather the individual character of a man or will you choose the road that will build and cultivate the true love that you were truly intended to have? Either way, the clock of your life ticks as you reflect on the depth of your desire to be a future wife.

Will you be the future wife who builds love based on status, possessions or wealth of a man or will you be the future wife who will commit to the endless possibilities that true love will bring?

Let the excitement begin as your mind explores the idea of being a future wife. I'm not referring to your best friend or any celebrity but you, yes there are billions of women on this earth but the DNA of you being a great future wife is within your reach.

Your heart has been shaped for that great man who can't wait to meet you.

#DearFutureWife,

I am here and I am so glad to be home with you. We've built something so special that it will inspire many others. I love you and thank God I made it to our house of love.

#YourFutureHusband

The Future

The journey of building true love is indeed a road many have traveled, yet the destination has never been reached. Every day, there are potential romantic relationships that begin and there are also romantic relationships that end.

Life is filled with great possibilities that will lead to triumph, happiness and fulfillment of true romantic love, however there is also the harsh reality that every romantic relationship may not evolve into perfect story that we've imagined or look like the scene from our favorite movie. Both the man and woman must truly examine their intentions for exploring the possibility of a romantic relationship between each other.

There must be a clear understanding that building true love will require, not only patience and time but the maturity of both that man and that woman to accomplish the goal of a successful yet fulfilling romantic connection.

It is often very difficult to determine the initial direction of a developing romantic relationship due to the various expectation the each man and each woman may have as well.

There is also the idea that each man and woman will bring certain fears into the potential romantic relationship based on previous relationship, desired qualities from a future mate and even the various opinions of family members and close friends.

The goals of each romantic relationship should be not only successfully reach marriage but have a successful marriage in the future.

The purpose of marriage is for the two individuals, a man and woman to grow together and become one unit, one team with the goal of walking together as each of them will experience changes throughout the duration of each other's lives.

While the pursuit of marriage is exciting and memorable, there will also be the discovery of the powerful element that each person regardless of marital status must truly realize, that each individual must be committed process of maturity.

Maturity is not defined by appearance, prestige or even level of income, it is the difference between potential and actual growth of individual. Maturity is a combination of life experience and wisdom learned throughout and individual's life.

Maturity is indeed a very important element in the growth or decline of a potential romantic relation.

Each man has a great responsibility to make a wise choice of who he will spend the rest of his life lead by his heavenly father. Marriage is not defined by the events of one day that is celebrated as a milestone each year but it is defined on how well that man and that woman choose to walk with each other each day.

Both the man and the woman must make a daily to decision to uphold the standards that will exhibit a healthy, fulfilling marriage covenant. From the very beginning both the man and woman establish to uphold the vows they have made to one another.

A vow is, solemn promise, pledge or personal commitment by an individual toward another individual to fulfill the responsibility of a prior promise or covenant made. The strength of a romantic relationship is determined by the vow that is established between that man and that woman.

The vow cannot be based on expectations of tangible elements such as health, beauty or even financial wealth, it should be based on intangible elements such as honesty, integrity, commitment and consistency. In our current society, it is evident that marriage is no longer held to a higher standard but rather a preparation for a day of celebration but not real preparation of the life after the marriage ceremony has concluded.

As you have chosen to read this book to this point, truly ask yourself if you truly desire to walk toward the covenant of marriage or is marriage just about the wedding day.

While social media can indeed paint the beautiful story of relationships, engagement and the wedding day, it also does not reveal the true journey that will include differences, issues and the establishment of the foundation that is needed for a romantic relationship to blossom into a successful marriage that goes beyond the wedding day.

For those who read this book and may ask the question of whether your current relationship will reach the ultimate goal of marriage, ask yourself this question, Have both you and your significant other determined that marriage is the goal or is it assumed that because the relationship has continued for a certain amount of time that marriage is the next step?

Is there trust, is this relationship based on true expectations or expectations of the culture such as media and entertainment. Even couples who begin relationship can fall subject to false expectations that is put upon by each other or even placed upon them by family and or friends.

Questions to ask yourself and your significant others:

Can I see myself with this person for the rest of my life?

What are my issues and how am I choosing to address them?

Have I forgiven those who hurt me in the past?

Have I established the expectations in this relationship or have I just assumed that those expectations will be met based on the length of the current relationship?

Do you feel pressure about making the step of marriage or are you excited about the idea of spending your life with this person?

Are you selfish? Are you willing to compromise in order to be unified?

Are you impatient?

Have you and your significant other set relationship goals?

Questions for those who are desire a future romantic relationship:

What issues do you current have that could potential be a barrier to the future success of a romantic relationship?

What do you consider your type? What do you consider your non-negotiables or things you will not tolerate no matter who the individual is?

How long do you desire to be in a relationship before considering marriage to that individual?

Do you both share the same belief in God?

Are you truly over your past relationships?

Are you selfish?

Are you argumentative?

What is one area that you know you need help?

How do you handle your finances?

#DearFutureWife,

Thank you for the joy you will bring to my life. You are indeed everything that I imagined, this has been an amazing journey and I look forward to growing with you for the rest of our lives.

#YourFutureHusband

Whether you've been inspired, challenged or begin to examine whether you are truly ready to embark upon the journey of true love, let the words of this book give you hope that the possibilities are endless as long as you keep in mind that journey will require you to grow in every area of your life. Just imagine, the day you stand before the altar beginning the wonderful journey of marriage.

Marriage doesn't begin on the wedding day, it begins the moment that you decide to do what others have failed to do and learn what it will take for your relationship to succeed.

Your future romantic relationship will look nothing like the movies you've seen, the music you've listened to or even resemble the relationships you consider as a model to follow after.

Your journey to toward true love will represent the work that is deemed necessary to set the relationship with your significant other apart from the other relationships that you will see from the outside looking in. Rest assure that as you continue to mature, your point of view towards true love will grow hopeful, optimistic and success will follow.

Remember, God has placed something special inside of every woman that the right man will recognize and will cherish, he will choose you not because of your physical features, or your social status but he will look into your eyes and see that the rest of his life is so much better with you then without you.

As you strive forward toward the journey of becoming a future wife, it begins with recognizing that you are worthy of being a wife, now the question will make a commitment to grow or will you just accept the idea that you are entitled to become a wife because you feel you deserve it.

The time is now don't just be a wife but be the best wife for the best man and become the great legacy that God intended for you to be.

#DearFutureWife,

Come forth your time is NOW!!!!.

www.ingramcontent.com/pod-product-compliance
Lightning Source LLC
Chambersburg PA
CBHW071058090426
42737CB00013B/2375